WEYK GLOBAL
BOOK SERIES

ZACHARY LUKASIEWICZ

WEYK GLOBAL MEDIA
Lincoln, Nebraska
www.weykglobal.com

Related Courses & Workshops: WeykGlobal.com
LinkedIn: linkedin.com/in/zdrake2013
More about the author: weykglobal.com/leadership
Please send errors, comments, and speaking inquiries to
hey@weykglobal.com

The goal in releasing this book series is to help narrow the gap between professional marketers and industry newcomers. The idea here is to provide necessary information to passionate individuals to make their business dreams a reality. Our marketing materials - including our courses and workshops - are all aligned on this front.

For Whom Is This Book Intended?

This book is meant for start-ups and small businesses that lack marketing-savvy staff but have a need to intelligently expand the reach of their goods or services. These companies may not have the budget to hire external marketing help, and may also find traditional Google tools to be intimidating. We seek to educate and demystify the online marketplace for these organizations.

What Does It Do?

Using a series of lessons, case studies, and quizzes (if you opt for our online courses), this book and its entire series guides you through 3-5 minute story-based chapters on search marketing, content marketing, PR & Media and more. All in all, we cover eighteen different topics. Depending on your sense of humor, our case studies can cause a few chuckles as you think about, for example, how Connor the karaoke rental equipment guy should improve his search results.

The lessons in this book are heavy on strategy and light on execution. Though this book helps readers differentiate between marketing tactics and identify the best strategies for different businesses, it does not go so far as to provide a detailed walk-through of execution using Google tools. That said, it certainly provides enough information to begin taking steps in the right direction.

How Does It Do It?

This book handles dry topics well, making consistency paramount. This keeps readers engaged in the lessons, with no time to lose focus.

Not only highly interactive, the chapters are also very brief at 3-5 minutes. There are also notes about various courses and workshops to help reinforce the takeaways.

Recommending This Book

Reviewing all of the chapters takes less than 45 minutes. As a digital marketing instructor for Growth(X) Academy, I integrate these essentials into my lessons on search marketing and content marketing in order to reinforce concepts.

WHY A BUSINESS EMAIL ADDRESS IS GOOD FOR BUSINESS

- What's the difference between a business email address and a personal one?
- Why should I have a business email address?
- How do I get a business email address?

Imagine you own a home that's overdue for a paint job. You've been meaning to paint it yourself, but finally admit you need to hire someone to do it for you.

You head down to your local hardware store and post a "House Painter Wanted" ad on the communal bulletin board. The next day, you check your email and see you already have 2 responses to your ad.

The first thing you notice is the applicants' email addresses. One seems way more trustworthy than the other, so you only reply to that address. But which one was it?

A business email address is one that's solely dedicated to business communication, and ends in a company's domain name (@antoniopainting.com).

Having a business email address seems like a minor detail, but it can have a huge effect on your business. For example, it helps boost your company's credibility by making your email communications look professional and legitimate.

A business email address also makes your company's emails more consistent. When every single one of your employees uses the same business domain in their email addresses, it's clear that you're all on the same, unified team.

The connection between your business email address and your website domain can raise brand awareness, too. Every time you and your team members email someone, your address will remind them of the company you represent.

You don't need to be a company with multiple employees to get a business email address. It's easy and affordable for businesses of all sizes.

Even if you are the only employee of your business, you can create multiple email addresses that will handle different business communications: info@antoniopainting.com, sales@antoniopainting.com, book@antoniopainting.com.

As your company grows, you can easily add email addresses for new employees. Or, if an employee leaves, you can still receive messages sent to their business email address.

TIP
What if you've been using a personal email address and it's well known to your customers? It's still a good idea to switch to a business address.

You can automatically forward messages to your new business address.

It's easy to get a business email address with Google's G Suite. Just go to google.com/gsuite to get started.

First, make sure you have a business domain name (AKA the address for your website). If you don't have a registered domain name, you can get one while setting up your G Suite account.

Then, fill in your information: your name, current email address, your business name, number of employees, and what country you're based in. Once you've done that, G Suite will take it from there.

DO THIS NOW

Yes, getting a business email address is straightforward. But there are a few steps you can do to make the process even easier. Let's create a to-do list to help.

If you're participating in the course, go to the next section to access your self assessment.

KEY TAKEAWAYS

1. A business email address is dedicated to business communication only and is connected to your business website's domain.
2. A business email address can improve your company's credibility, makes your communication more consistent, and can boost brand awareness.
3. Visit google.com/gsuite to set up a business email address, and then from there you can register a domain name or use one you already have.

KEEP CUSTOMERS INTERESTED WITH EMAIL AUTOMATION

- What is email automation?
- How can I use it to help my business?
- How does it help my customers stay interested and engaged?

Email automation. Not the warmest-sounding subject out there, right? But let's look at it in a different way.

Email automation is like a large party where everyone is mingling and getting to know each other.

Your marketing emails should be like a chat with that great conversationalist: flowing, engaging, and relevant to the people involved.

But instead of the guests at one party, you might have thousands of customers – each with different interests and needs.

On top of that, you probably want to talk to all these customers over an extended amount of time. How can you possibly handle it all? Email automation.

Email automation happens when you set up a series of programmed, timely emails that are triggered by certain customer actions. Sometimes it's called drip marketing.

It can help you turn potential customers into actual ones, keep your current customers active, and get former customers to be all up in your business again.

But Primer, you ask (or don't ask, but bear with us), is it really possible to send unique messages to certain customers without writing to each and every single customer myself?

Let's check out how Custom Service Hardware (CSH) did it. They're an online retailer that sells supplies to people remodeling their homes.

CSH noticed a lot of customers abandoned their online shopping carts before hitting "purchase," so they used email automation to turn these lapsed customers into active ones.

If customers abandoned their cart for over an hour, CSH emailed them and offered to help complete the order – along with a 5% discount expiring in 7 days.

If they didn't act after the 1st email, they'd get another 7 days later that reminded them the coupon was expiring. CSH also asked if they had any questions, which put the customers first.

This email automation campaign ended up being a great success for CSH. Let's check out how customers responded to the initial email that had the 5% discount code and the follow-up email a week later.

Here's how the 1st email did:

OPEN RATE
58.7% of customers opened it.

CLICK-THROUGH RATE
Of those customers, 37% then clicked through to their shopping carts.

PURCHASES
36.6% of those who clicked through then bought the products in their carts.

Here's how the 2nd did:

OPEN RATE
40.9% of customers opened it.

CLICK-THROUGH RATE
Of those customers, 22.2% then clicked through to their shopping carts.

PURCHASES
100% of those who clicked through then bought the products in their carts.

LISTEN UP
Just like Custom Service Hardware focused on re-engaging lapsed customers, it's important that you figure out what your goal is and how to reach it before you start email automation.

Reaching your email automation goal works like this: The customer takes an action. The action triggers emails (called an email flow). Each email is sent at a certain cadence. These emails help you reach your goal. Let's explore this by looking at some common goals.

The first popular goal is onboarding, or teaching customers how to use your product or service.

The trigger for that goal is customers visiting your site, app, or store and signing up for your emails or making a purchase.

Here's a possible onboarding email flow: The customer buys one of your products and an hour later they get your welcome email. Over the next few days, they'll receive your "how my product works" email.

Another goal is engagement, or encouraging customers to interact with your products or business even more.

The trigger is when customers try some of your features or services on your app or site, but not others.

You can set up your email automation flow like this: Every few weeks, those customers will get an email encouraging them to engage with your business (by taking a specific action of your choice).

Every month, your newsletter will be emailed to them. And periodically, they'll receive emails about your new features or products you're launching, and/or tips and tricks.

Retention – or getting customers to stay loyal and keep coming back – is also a common goal.

For this goal, you can use different triggers and email flows. For example, let's say the trigger is a customer making their first purchase. Two days later, they'll receive an email asking for feedback.

If a customer makes more purchases, that's also a trigger. A day later they can get an email with related products they might like.

You might also consider reengagement as a goal. It's getting a user who's stopped using your product to start using it again.

The trigger is when customers forget about you and have stopped participating completely. For example, let's say they haven't visited your site or used your app in a while.

For a set time period, you can have them receive emails every 7 days. The 1st can be a "we miss you" email. The 2nd, a "what you're missing out on" message. Finally, they'll be sent a discount or promotion.

TIP
Your email flows shouldn't overwhelm or annoy people. Also, let people opt-in and out of your emails.

DO THIS NOW
Let's find out what you need to do to get yourself and your site or app ready for email automation.

If you're participating in the course, go to the next section to access your self assessment.

KEY TAKEAWAYS
1. Email automation is a series of timed emails that are triggered by customer actions.
2. It can help you reach goals - like onboarding new customers and keeping customers engaged.
3. A series of emails should be sent with the right cadence.

GET TO THE POINT: TIPS FOR CRAFTING EFFECTIVE EMAILS

- How can effective email communication help my business and brand?
- How can I craft effective emails?
- How can I make sure I'm responding to emails properly?

You've probably heard the saying, "It's not what you say, but how you say it." And that's definitely true for all business communication, including emails.

Emails lack body language and tone of voice. That's why you have to make them clear, relevant, and appropriate. Otherwise, you might end up with a communication breakdown between you and the people you're sending emails to.

Let's explore this by imagining that account executive Alex emails brand manager Barbara to recap their meeting about a new campaign they're launching.

Alex composes 2 different versions of the email.

Taking the time to carefully craft emails is important because email can be a powerful tool for communicating with your colleagues and customers.

Emails are also easily shared. People can save your message or forward it on to anyone. That's why it's vital to avoid sending inappropriate or irrelevant emails that could spread like a viral meme, hurting your brand.

Fortunately, there are steps you can take to make sure your email communications work hard to strengthen your relationships and to positively impact your brand's marketing efforts.

To craft your email, first be clear about its purposes. Emails can be about anything, but they usually fulfill 1 of 2 purposes: to inform or to confirm.

To inform can mean recapping a meeting, providing status updates, sharing a document, or making an introduction.

To confirm can mean verifying an appointment, asking for information from a colleague, or reaching out to a vendor for a price estimate.

To get the response you're looking for, make sure your call to action is clear. For example, if you want to set up a meeting, you might write: "Please let me know if this date works. Or let me know when you're available."

Once you have a clear purpose, do a quick gut check: Is email really the best way to communicate that purpose?

If your purpose is urgent, email might not be an effective format. People sometimes check their email inboxes sporadically or infrequently. So, if it's urgent, make a phone call or talk in person.

Also, email isn't ideal for issues needing detailed discussions, like extensive brainstorming or feedback. Emailing back and forth can slow the flow of ideas. It can also make it hard to ask follow-up questions or give clear, concise remarks.

When it comes to difficult or sticky situations, email is no replacement for honest in-person conversation. Email might save you an awkward conversation up front, but it can lead to confusion and feelings of resentment in the future.

LISTEN UP

So you've decided your purpose is email-worthy. How do you craft an effective message?

Good news: You don't have to be Shakespeare. You just need to know how to get your point across.

Lastly, email isn't the best way to share private or sensitive information. Emails are not secure, and can be forwarded to anyone, anywhere, without you knowing it.

Start by making sure that your email is short and to the point.

If you spent all afternoon typing out an email that now reads like a Charles Dickens novel, make edits and create an abridged version. Keep in mind that there's a high likelihood your recipient will be reading the email on his or her phone.

To make sure your email is succinct enough, quickly scan it and see if you can pull out all the main points. You might consider using bullet points or numbered lists to highlight important points.

Next, make sure to use an appropriate tone of voice. When you're writing a business email, you're representing your brand or company.

Adjust your tone according to the recipient. Writing a reprimanding email to a delinquent vendor or employee might help them respect your priorities. Sending a strongly-worded email to your CEO might not be a good idea.

When writing emails to customers or contacts on your marketing email lists, make sure the language is consistent with your brand's tone of voice, even if it's a shipping confirmation or a password reset email.

The words you choose to use can also affect the tone of your email. Don't use any that accidentally weaken your message and purpose.

Words and phrases like "Yes, but," "actually," "sorry," "kind of," "in my opinion," or "I'm no expert" might seem like harmless fillers, but they're actually "shrinkers," which can make your emails, purpose, and even you, seem weak.

Also, phrases like "I think," "I believe," and "I feel" can make you seem indecisive. If you're giving your opinion, provide a reason for your decision and your thinking behind it, and open it up to a conversation.

For example, instead of "I don't think this color works," say, "The green does not align with our brand style guide. Please refer to it for color selection purposes."

On the other hand, make sure not to come off as overly aggressive. You may think that writing in ALL CAPS or using exclamation points emphasizes your opinion, but to your recipients it may come off as angry.

DO THIS NOW
Take a moment to think about all the "shrinker" words you have a habit of using. Let's create a list of your worst offenders so you can remind yourself to avoid them from now on.

If you're participating in the course, go to the next section to access your self assessment.

KEY TAKEAWAYS
1. To get your point across and get the response you're looking for, your emails should be succinct, relevant, and appropriate.
2. You're emails should have a clear purpose, express your expectations, and have a call to action.
3. Avoid using "shrinker" words and other phrases that might make your emails seem weak and indecisive.

THE NON-SPAMMY WAY TO BUILD AN EMAIL LIST

- Why is building an email or newsletter subscriber list important?
- How can I help people understand the value in signing up for my emails or newsletters?
- How can I use my online content to convince people to sign up?

Imagine you're at a business conference, networking like a pro. You meet someone who seems like a great contact to have in the future.

But you wait too long to ask for their business card and lose them in the crowd of people rushing to get free conference T-shirts. It's a lost opportunity. Now, imagine this situation is about your business engaging with a new customer.

If you don't ask to keep in touch with the customer, you might lose the chance to reach out to them later. However, if you ask for their email address at the right moment, you can add them to your email marketing list. But is email marketing really worth all that effort?

In order to do email marketing, you need to build an email list of current and potential customers who'd welcome seeing your business in their inboxes.

Buying a pre-populated email list might be tempting. But, think about how you feel when you get unsolicited emails from random people or companies. Not great, right? You most likely hit the Trash or Spam button.

So, you don't want your business to be seen as a nuisance and put on the dreaded spam list. That's why it's best to build your email list organically – AKA, get the people you engage with to say, "Yes, I'd love to hear from you again."

TIP
The content of your emails is a hugely important part of getting people to sign up and not unsubscribe. Emails are valuable when they're useful, timely, or interesting to recipients. For example: exclusive discounts, holiday gift reminders, relevant tips and tricks, etc.

Getting people to sign up for your list is a bit like being a salesperson for your emails. You need to communicate their value quickly and persuasively.

What are the benefits of receiving your emails? How can you put those benefits into calls to action (CTAs) that would encourage sign ups? For example: "What's for dinner? Get delicious, easy recipes delivered straight to your inbox."

Make sure your CTAs stay true to your brand voice and personality, and try not to get too pushy. Let people know that it's okay for them to say no. Make sure you include both a "Sign Up" button and a "No Thanks" or "Sign Up Later" button.

Put the same amount of thought into the forms you'll use to collect people's email addresses. They can be a make-it-or-break-it moment for your email list.

Make it as easy and as streamlined as possible for people to give you their information. Instead of sending them to another page when they click your sign up button, let them enter their emails on the same screen as your CTA.

Also, don't ask for too much information. The more boxes people have to fill out, the less likely they are to finish the form. Yes, ask for their name and email address, but maybe leave out "What city do you live in?" and "What's your spirit animal?"

TOOLS
Email list and newsletter managing tools like Mailchimp and Constant Contact usually have form builders that you can customize and then embed on your site and other online properties.

When you have your CTAs and forms ready, you can have them appear in a variety of locations and at different times, and then test what works best.

Some locations you can try are your site's homepage and product pages, a sidebar and splash screen on your blog, and your social media pages.

Also play around with the most effective moments for your CTA to appear. For example: when someone finishes reading your blog post, when they create a profile on your site, or when they complete a purchase.

To help see which mixtures of CTA message, location, and timing are most effective, you can do A/B testing – which is pitting different combinations against each other to see which ones win out (get the most email list sign ups).

REMEMBER
You want to deliver the right message in the right place at the right time. Let people fall in love with you before you propose. A new site visitor may not understand your business' value yet, so having your CTA appear the moment they land on your homepage might not be effective.

Of course, your CTAs can only succeed if people are engaging with your site, blogs, and social media activity – which is where content strategy comes in.

A good content strategy can draw people to your site, blogs, and social media profiles, help them appreciate what they see there, and encourage them to sign up for more (AKA get on your email list).

By content, we mean articles, posts, whitepapers, infographics, etc. Just like your emails, they should be useful, timely, or interesting to your audience. A smart strategy is to have your emails link to this content on your site or blog.

You can also try social media strategies. Use social media to spread your content and get people interested. Then ask them to sign up for your email list. You can even embed an email sign up form into your social media posts.

As a general rule, check with your legal department or a lawyer to make sure you're complying with email marketing laws in the area your business is operating in.

DO THIS NOW
Like we mentioned before, email marketing can be fast and relatively easy to set up. To help, let's create a to do list of steps you can take to prep yourself.

If you're participating in the course, go to the next section to access your self assessment.

KEY TAKEAWAYS
1. An email list helps you reach out to customers in the future and keep them engaged with your business.
2. Encourage people to sign up for and stay on your email list by having strong email content and by using strong CTAs that describe why your emails are so valuable.
3. A content strategy for your website, blog, and social media activity can help draw people in and convince them to sign up for more.

MAKE EMAIL MARKETING YOUR SECRET WEAPON

- Why should I do email marketing?
- What types of emails can I send?
- What are the best ways to measure my email marketing's success?

It's easy to take email for granted. It's something that's almost too available, you use it fairly often, you have it at work and at home... Wait. Let's think about that.

How many times have you checked your email today? Once? Twice?

Are you checking it right now?

Email marketing is great for a lot of reasons, but here are 4 good ones...

Email marketing connects you directly with your customers. People's inboxes are often their "To Do" lists – and your email can be part of that list.

You can also get really targeted. It's possible to send a different message and different call to action to every single contact you have.

It's pretty easy to set up and get going quickly. A lot of businesses use it as one of their first marketing channels.

Lastly, it's easy to tell if you're reaching your marketing goals. Tracking email engagement rates helps you figure out if your email marketing is working.

TIP
To set your email marketing up for success, think of any email you send as a nice bonus for your customers.

That means every email you send needs to offer something valuable to the person reading it.

Valuable emails are useful, timely, or interesting to people. Let's check out how a real business did it right.

This useful email from wedding registry site Zola gave engaged couples insider tips and valuable advice from recently married couples.

It's safe to say that Valentine's Day is highly relevant to engaged couples. And with V-Day comes forgetting to buy a gift for V-Day. So Zola sent a timely email with last minute gift ideas.

A lot of wedding gifts have one use only. A cake stand, for example. But Zola found interesting ways to make them multi-use and emailed those ideas to their customers.

Okay, great, you can create some useful, timely, and interesting emails like Zola did, hit send, and ride off into the sunset, right?

Sure...as long as that sunset includes the golden glow of measuring your email marketing success.

You can measure a lot, but let's look at these 4:

CLICK-THROUGH RATE (CTR)
% of people who clicked on your email links

CONVERSION RATE
% of people taking the action your email asked them to do

OPEN RATE

% of people who opened your email

UNSUBSCRIBE RATE
% of people who decided to unsubscribe after getting your email

Why are we looking at them? Because 2 of them are the most important email marketing rates to measure, and 2 of them aren't that crucial.

Let's see if you can guess which ones are which.

CTR tells you if your emails are useful, timely, or interesting enough.

You can also measure how your CTR changes over time to know when you should update or tweak your email content.

Tracking it will show you if your message or offer can successfully get people to click your links and learn more.

Conversion rate tells you if your email marketing is helping your business.

A potential customer becomes a "conversion" when they take the ultimate action you wanted them to take, like buying a last-minute Valentine's Day gift from your online store.

Conversion rate, then, is one of the most important things to track if you want to know how much your email marketing is helping you reach your goals.

Open and unsubscribe rates are unreliable.

An email is only counted as opened if the person also gets the images embedded in the email. Unfortunately, a lot of people have automatic image blocking.

You also can't tell how many people actually unsubscribed, as a lot of them don't bother using your unsubscribe button. They'll just stop opening or reading your emails, or send them to the spam folder.

DO THIS NOW

Even if you're not quite ready to launch a full email marketing campaign, you can start thinking about the types of useful, timely, or interesting emails that could work for your business.

If you're participating in the course, go to the next section to access your self assessment.

KEY TAKEAWAYS
1. Email marketing is an easy way to reach customers and achieve your business goals.
2. Every email you send should be useful, timely, or interesting.
3. Click-through rate and conversion rate are the 2 most important things to track.

BUILD YOUR EMAIL MARKETING A-TEAM

- Why should I consider hiring a team to do my email marketing?
- What should I look for when hiring people for my team?
- What are the core roles and responsibilities of an email marketing team?

Email marketer, email specialist, email manager, email marketing strategist. Aren't all these job titles for people who send out marketing emails?

Actually, these people make sure that email is an integral part of your marketing, that it drives sales to your business, and that whatever you send out is part of a bigger strategy.

It's important to have people who make sure all these things get done because email marketing can be incredibly hardworking and effective.

Before you start calling marketing headhunters, set clear goals for what you want to achieve.

There are 3 types of email marketing goals:

ACQUISITION
Build your subscriber list and send emails that encourage action.

RETENTION
Keep existing customers interested and engaged.

AWARENESS
Get your brand in front of as many people as possible.

Your email marketing efforts should support your overall business goals. This will help ensure your messaging is consistent and is right for your target audience.

The type of people you hire will depend on your email marketing goals.

If your goal is acquisition, look for candidates who are nimble and are skilled at writing copy that drives subscriptions and sales.

If your goal is retention, look for candidates who are comfortable segmenting customers, setting metrics, doing analysis, and who know how to craft emails to meet specific needs.

If your goal is awareness, look for storytellers who can write engaging copy that ties into your brand voice, catches people's attention, and makes headlines.

LISTEN UP
A team doesn't have to mean hiring a whole platoon. You could bring in a writer, or a designer, or a strategist, or all 3. You could even manage the email marketing yourself. (Yes, there can be an "I" in team.)

Successful email marketers are great communicators and curious researchers.

Having a writer on board is helpful. But if you don't have one, make sure the marketer who is assigned to the role is a good editor.

When reviewing candidates, have them show previous campaigns they've worked on and ask them about their thinking behind the process. Also, have them present ideas on how to improve your marketing.

You might want to ask the candidates to run a test campaign. When reviewing these tests, pay close attention to their ability to write engaging subject lines, maintain brand voice, and use effective calls to action (CTA).

Once hired and onboarded, the first task of your shiny, new email marketing team is to develop a shiny, new email marketing strategy.

Creating a strategy is a bit like wearing bifocal glasses: It's being able to look at short-term goals, long-term goals, and considering how your email marketing activity ties into your brand's overall revenue goals.

When developing a strategy, the team should think about how to manage different email lists, how to approach campaigns with different goals, and how to balance those along with triggered messages and transactional emails.

To do this role effectively, your team needs to analyze the strategy, look at what's working, and what needs to be improved. Then they need to communicate these learnings and suggest changes based on the data they gathered.

REMEMBER
Keep in mind that no matter how much you plan or who you hire, they might not get everything correct 100% of the time.

Give them the freedom to adjust, experiment, and make changes that can improve the strategy.

In addition to thinking about the bigger picture strategy, your email marketing team needs to know how to handle day-to-day operations.

Your team should create a content calendar with weekly emails, release dates, product launches, and special events. Review the calendar with them once a week to see if they're on the right track, and adjust if changes are needed.

Test emails before they send them out to actual customers. Services like Litmus let you see how your emails look on different devices so you can preview them before hitting send.

Also, to make sure your emails are going to customers and not to spam folders, your team should be up to date on how spam filters work.

DO THIS NOW
Now that you've learned what to think about when building an email marketing team, let's see if it's time for you to assemble your own A-team.

If you're participating in the course, go to the next section to access your self assessment.

KEY TAKEAWAYS
1. There are 3 main goals for email marketing: acquisition, retention, and awareness.
2. To make sure your email marketing does into your overall business goals, develop an email marketing strategy.
3. When hiring, look for marketers who are good communicators and curious researchers.

BUILD YOUR EMAIL MARKETING A-TEAM

- Why should I consider hiring a team to do my email marketing?
- What should I look for when hiring people for my team?
- What are the core roles and responsibilities of an email marketing team?

Email marketer, email specialist, email manager, email marketing strategist. Aren't all these job titles for people who send out marketing emails?

Actually, these people make sure that email is an integral part of your marketing, that it drives sales to your business, and that whatever you send out is part of a bigger strategy.

It's important to have people who make sure all these things get done because email marketing can be incredibly hardworking and effective.

Before you start calling marketing headhunters, set clear goals for what you want to achieve.

There are 3 types of email marketing goals:

ACQUISITION
Build your subscriber list and send emails that encourage action.

RETENTION
Keep existing customers interested and engaged.

AWARENESS
Get your brand in front of as many people as possible.

Your email marketing efforts should support your overall business goals. This will help ensure your messaging is consistent and is right for your target audience.

The type of people you hire will depend on your email marketing goals.

If your goal is acquisition, look for candidates who are nimble and are skilled at writing copy that drives subscriptions and sales.

If your goal is retention, look for candidates who are comfortable segmenting customers, setting metrics, doing analysis, and who know how to craft emails to meet specific needs.

If your goal is awareness, look for storytellers who can write engaging copy that ties into your brand voice, catches people's attention, and makes headlines.

LISTEN UP
A team doesn't have to mean hiring a whole platoon. You could bring in a writer, or a designer, or a strategist, or all 3. You could even manage the email marketing yourself. (Yes, there can be an "I" in team.)

Successful email marketers are great communicators and curious researchers.

Having a writer on board is helpful. But if you don't have one, make sure the marketer who is assigned to the role is a good editor.

When reviewing candidates, have them show previous campaigns they've worked on and ask them about their thinking behind the process. Also, have them present ideas on how to improve your marketing.

You might want to ask the candidates to run a test campaign. When reviewing these tests, pay close attention to their ability to write engaging subject lines, maintain brand voice, and use effective calls to action (CTA).

Once hired and onboarded, the first task of your shiny, new email marketing team is to develop a shiny, new email marketing strategy.

Creating a strategy is a bit like wearing bifocal glasses: It's being able to look at short-term goals, long-term goals, and considering how your email marketing activity ties into your brand's overall revenue goals.

When developing a strategy, the team should think about how to manage different email lists, how to approach campaigns with different goals, and how to balance those along with triggered messages and transactional emails.

To do this role effectively, your team needs to analyze the strategy, look at what's working, and what needs to be improved. Then they need to communicate these learnings and suggest changes based on the data they gathered.

REMEMBER
Keep in mind that no matter how much you plan or who you hire, they might not get everything correct 100% of the time.

Give them the freedom to adjust, experiment, and make changes that can improve the strategy.

In addition to thinking about the bigger picture strategy, your email marketing team needs to know how to handle day-to-day operations.

Your team should create a content calendar with weekly emails, release dates, product launches, and special events. Review the calendar with them once a week to see if they're on the right track, and adjust if changes are needed.

Test emails before they send them out to actual customers. Services like Litmus let you see how your emails look on different devices so you can preview them before hitting send.

Also, to make sure your emails are going to customers and not to spam folders, your team should be up to date on how spam filters work.

DO THIS NOW
Now that you've learned what to think about when building an email marketing team, let's see if it's time for you to assemble your own A-team.

If you're participating in the course, go to the next section to access your self assessment.

KEY TAKEAWAYS
1. There are 3 main goals for email marketing: acquisition, retention, and awareness.
2. To make sure your email marketing does into your overall business goals, develop an email marketing strategy.
3. When hiring, look for marketers who are good communicators and curious researchers.

GET YOUR EMAILS IN SHAPE WITH MULTIVARIATE TESTING

- How is multivariate testing different from A/B testing?
- Why should I use it in my email marketing?
- How do I do multivariate testing?

Imagine Katie owns Kangaroo Kickboxing, a business that offers martial arts and self defense classes.

Thanks to her great workouts, she's built up a large email subscriber list that's made up of current customers and other people who want to learn more about Kangaroo Kickboxing.

Katie decides to open a second Kangaroo Kickboxing on the other side of town so she can increase her customer base. She knows email marketing will be key to getting the word out and filling her new studio with people.

After brainstorming what the email content should be, she narrows it down to a couple different images and calls to action (CTAs).

She's been playing with different combinations, but isn't sure which will be the most effective.

Multivariate testing is a lot like A/B testing after it's gone through

Kangaroo Kickboxing strength training.

While A/B testing can only work with one element at a time, multivariate testing can evaluate different, more complex combinations of elements at the same time. For example, let's say Katie wants to test 2 CTAs with 4 different images.

With A/B testing, she'd first test which CTA worked best. Then, to find out which image worked best, she'd have to test each of them individually with her winning CTA.

Unfortunately, Katie might not get the most reliable results. For example, what if the combination of the losing CTA with the winning image would actually perform the best?

With multivariate testing, she could simultaneously test 8 different versions of her email (2 CTAs x 4 images) to see which combo worked best.

This testing method is fast, effective, and reliable, and can be incredibly valuable to those with large email lists. It even helps you with more than just the current email being tested. It improves all your future emails, too.

That's because the more of this testing you do, the more you'll know what works best for successfully marketing to your email subscriber list.

Multivariate testing can help you:

FIND TRENDS
For example, your audience might like drawings over photos.

OPTIMIZE CONTENT
Know how to tweak your copy and design to engage your audience.

STAY FOCUSED
No more guessing and hoping. Instead, create a smart game plan.

LISTEN UP

If A/B testing puts variables into a bracket tournament, then multivariate testing has variables going full fight club on each other. And the first rule of email fight club is: Don't talk about email fight club. Just kidding, it's: Choose your variables.

Services like MailChimp help you do multivariate testing, and most let you test up to 8 versions of your emails. That's a lot of variables you can throw into the ring.

Your variables might be what time you send your email, content, subject line, sender's name, background color, whether or not you include a photo of your new cat...basically, anything goes. Don't be afraid to get creative with your testing.

That being said, you should conduct focused, intentional tests based on hypotheses. For example: "I think customers will respond better to direct commands vs. gentle wooing. I'll test a pushy subject line against a subtler, more enticing one."

Even if multivariate testing proves your hypothesis wrong, it's still a win. You've just learned something new and valuable about your audience's preferences.

Okay, you've chosen your variables and now you're ready to test. But wait...did you give your email versions enough room and time to properly compete?

There's no definitive answer on how many subscribers you need or how long you should run your test. It depends on what you're testing (opens, clicks, or purchases) and how big of a change you're looking to find.

In general, you'll need a large enough testing pool to make sure your test results – and the decisions you make from them – represent a good amount of your audience.

And, you need to run your tests long enough for the right customer engagement data (clicks on links, sales on your website, etc.) to come in.

To help you figure out your testing pool size, you can use "sample size" calculators on sites like Optimizely and Qubit. As for test length, one rule of thumb is to conduct a test for at least 4 hours.

Once you've started running your tests, look for meaning in this multivariate world. That is, know what to look for in your results and how to interpret those insights.

On your testing service's report page, check out your combination results to see which mix of variables is most effective. This can help you discover insights like: "People hate this CTA and this image on their own, but love them together."

Next, look at results per variable. This tells you how much each individual variable affected your email's effectiveness across all combinations. That way you'll know if, for example, your CTA matters more than the image you chose.

Also, know what success looks like. Industry standards say a 20-30% open rate is generally the best indication of a strong email. However, if you're mainly testing your email's content, click rate is a good statistic to consider.

DO THIS NOW
In the spirit of testing, let's figure out how ready you are to do multivariate testing with a short, easy, no-big-deal self-evaluation.

If you're participating in the course, go to the next section to access your self assessment.

KEY TAKEAWAYS
1. Multivariate testing lets you evaluate different combinations of variables at the same time.
2. It can give you valuable insights into your audience's preferences that will help your future email marketing.
3. To do multivariate testing, choose variables, form hypotheses, have a large email list, and know how to inter-

pret your results.

REACH CUSTOMERS, NOT SPAM FILTERS

- What are spam filters?
- How and why should I avoid them?
- How can I keep my email contact list up-to-date and relevant?

As a marketer, getting customers to subscribe to your mailing list can be the beginning of a beautiful friendship. But, just like any relationship, it takes work.

Think about it: What if someone you don't know shows up at your door and says, "Hey, do you want to be friends? I bought a pizza." Even if you really like pizza you'd probably say, "Thanks but no thanks," and lock the door.

The same goes for users. If you indiscriminately send unsolicited emails with suspicious subject lines or messaging to large groups of people, AKA spam, their email servers will block you with their spam filters.

However, even if you're legit and only send marketing emails to users on your contact list, your emails might be blocked if the content seems generic or overused. Think of it like inbox intuition.

Imagine Wilbur's Watches sends out an e-blast with the subject line, "Our incredible sale is now on!!!" to their customers, announcing their holiday sale. Although they are a popular and legitimate brand, the email ends up in users' spam folders. Why?

Spam filters don't just block unwanted emails. They can also learn to detect different types of spam.

They do this by analyzing the email's content, subject lines, metadata, IP address, code, and format — among other things. For example, some spam filters can tell if the email's body text was dragged-and-dropped from a word processing program.

Also, it doesn't matter if users would be interested in the content of the email. If they didn't give you explicit permission to send them messages, it may be considered spam.

Spam filters are set up so people won't be bombarded with annoying or inappropriate messages, and to protect them from scammers. (Spoiler alert: That Nigerian prince isn't real.)

They also exist so legitimate businesses that don't spam aren't drowned out by imposters. However, this means that sometimes, despite your best intentions, your emails can get mistaken for spam.

So why don't spam filters tell marketers exactly what to avoid? Because if they did, they'd be unintentionally giving that information to spammers, too. However, there are things you can do to help your emails end up in the inbox.

The first step to making a connection is to get personal. If your email begins with "Dear valued customer," it'll trip the alarm.

Think about how it feels to get a text from a friend versus an unknown number. Well, spam filters can detect if you have friendly information like first or last names, and might flag emails if you don't include it.

Give users options as to what kinds of emails they want to receive. For instance, if you distribute a newsletter and lots of event invitations, ask users if they want to subscribe to both, or just one.

Use a "double opt-in" system: After a user has opted in, show them an exit screen that tells them you've sent them a confirmation email. In the email itself, ask the user to click a link to approve and finalize the opt-in.

Make the unsubscribe button or link easy to find in the email footer. Users might want a break from receiving your emails, so it's better to have them unsubscribe than to flag them. This helps keep communication channels open for the future.

LISTEN UP

Even if users give you their email addresses as part of a purchase, you can't send a marketing campaign message to those addresses because it will get flagged. Instead, send out an initial email from your personal account telling them about the campaign, and allowing them to opt in.

Spam filters analyze everything from content to formatting. Make sure your emails look professional and match your brand's style and identity.

After acquiring an email address, don't wait too long before starting communication. Send out an email right after the user has opted in, giving a sense of the types of content they should be expecting, like deals, news, and more.

Be consistent with your emails, and set expectations about their frequency and content. If you say you'll send a weekly email, sending one every day isn't cool.

Avoid using cliché subject lines, like "Click Here!" or "HURRY NOW!!!" On that note, don't write in ALL CAPS and avoid overusing exclamation points.

You can use HTML to make your emails stand out, but avoid creating emails that have big images, with little or no text. Spam filters don't read images, so they'll just assume you're an overachieving spammer.

TIP
Avoid using purchased lists of leads and emails.

These types of contact lists get passed around a lot, and most spam filters know how to detect them.

A true relationship is one that grows over time, so making a connection is only the first step — the next is maintaining and sustaining the relationship.

Internet service providers (ISP) can detect email inactivity. If your emails go unopened for too long, the ISP will label all emails from the forwarding address as spam.

If you notice inactivity from a user, reach out with a personalized message. Instead of sending them the next newsletter, send an email saying "Hey, haven't heard from you in a while. Just checking to see if you still want to get our emails."

Also, if a user doesn't engage with your emails within 6 months, their contact details go to what's called a "stale list." In that case, you'll need to send them a reconfirmation email, and ask them to opt in again.

Another way to avoid having your emails flagged is by monitoring and optimizing them.

If you're running an email marketing campaign, consider hiring an email marketing expert or consultant to give you stats and reports on the effectiveness of your emails.

In the report's overview page you can see complaints, AKA "abuse reports," and check email open rates. Industry standards say that you should aim for a 20-30% open rate, so if yours is lower, you should consider a change.

Check your "hard bounces" and SMTP (Simple Mail Transfer Protocol) replies. Hard bounces happen when the server hosting the email has blocked you entirely. SMTP replies indicate errors, which may include spam filter issues.

It's hard to get back into the inbox once your domain has been labeled as spam. That's why you should test your emails before you send them to actual users.

Set up test accounts with free email providers, like Gmail or Yahoo. If your emails aren't going through, try making some changes before resending. For example, remove a link or change the "from" address.

Avoid using the word "test" in the subject headline. Also, don't send the email to multiple people within the same company because it will be blocked by the company's firewall.

If you have a larger budget for email marketing, you can hire an email marketing service, like Mail Monitor or Return Path, to do testing and monitoring for you.

DO THIS NOW
Now that you've learned how to keep your marketing emails from ending up in spam folders, let's create a list of things to do next time you initiate an email campaign.

If you're participating in the course, go to the next section to access your self assessment.

KEY TAKEAWAYS
1. Spam filters block any email that look suspicious and irrelevant to the user.
2. To avoid having your emails and up in the spam folder, ask users to opt in to your mailing list.
3. To maintain your contacts, make sure your emails are tested, and that they are consistent in frequency and tone.

WEYK GLOBAL LEADERSHIP

Zachary Lukasiewicz is the Managing Director of Weyk Global.

Originally from Omaha, Nebraska and attended Drake University in Des Moines, Iowa. He served as a tri-chair for the Human Capital committee of Capital Crossroads, the 10-year plan for Central Iowa, where he focused on the attraction and retention of Des Moines residents from cradle to career.

Zachary has operated 50+ accelerator assistance programs and in-house workshops, and staffed marketing teams around the globe.

Zachary's focus is marketing investment - sourcing the best talent, recruiting domain experts and executing on his proven playbook and delivering the best possible experience. He sets the strategic direction and client profile within the program, including a curated team of mentors, investors and business advisors.

Zachary is responsible for making the initial relationships. He takes overall ownership of each programs' success and partners with other operations units external to Weyk Global to ensure exceptional delivery of exceptional marketing programs, and is ultimately responsible for turning good companies into great ones.

Additional:

- Builds systems around market research and data-driven management—especially in budget allocation, paid/organic, and navigating complex customer cadences.
- Experience building marketing infrastructure and communication processes throughout US Techstars classes, reducing acquisition costs with greater capacity and cost-effectiveness
- A recognized expert on US social media in real estate, education, and human resources industries
- A leader with proven skills working with innovative teams to build customer consensus and drive buy-in behavior across purpose-driven organizations
- Motivates large organizations and individual personnel to award-winning performance and achievement
- Leadership experience encompasses direct management of 20+ personnel, over $8.5 million in assets/budgets with a record of five enterprise acquisitions and assisting in seven fundraising rounds

Zachary has served as a management consultant with startups backed by White Star Capital, Hoxton Ventures, Bloomberg Beta, Real Ventures, BDC Capital, Chris Anderson. Eduardo Gentil, Jacqueline Novogratz, Mehdi Alhassani, Ana Carolina, Entrepreneur, Obvious Ventures, MIT, Ittleson Foundation, J.M.Kaplan Fund, SC/E, MassCEC, WhiteHouse.gov, ServiceCorps, The One Foundation, The Godley Family Foundation, the Boston Foundation, Boris Jabes, Ilya

Sukhar, Chris DeVore, Alex Payne, DJF, Liquid 2 Ventures, GSF, Sanjay Jain, Felix Anthony, Uma Raghavan, and TiE LaunchPad. Zachary's early experience comes from working under business leaders at market-leading companies including ISoft Data Systems, LukeUSA, AlphaPrep.net, Staffing Nerd, Immun.io, Reflect.io, Validated.co, Shaun White Enterprises, Solstice.us, Swym, Staffing Robot, Hatchlings, Coaching Actuaries, 8 to Great, Target, Paylease, MidAmerican Energy, and R&R Realty Group.

Weyk Global offers two types of in-house training:

- Our workshops at any location:
All advertised courses can be taught in the location of your choice at a time convenient for you. We will ensure the course is specific to your business and sector.

- Our workshops tailored to your needs:
We can design bespoke training to meet the needs of your business. You can provide a brief or we will work with you to develop the training resources to help you achieve your goals.

Analytics Fundamentals

Discover the fundamentals of analytics and the different tools that will help you draw insights from analytics.

In this workshop, we'll examine the fundamentals of analytics, exploring the tools and their most appropriate use. You'll discover how to draw insights from analytics, enabling you to predict emerging trends. This course is designed for those who are curious in nature, enjoy problem-solving and prefer a self- learning, exploratory approach to knowledge.

Career Accelerator

Ensure you have the skills and knowledge to quickly start making an impact in your organization.

Getting into the industry is always challenging; university provides many of the concepts but not necessarily all the skills to be really ready to make a difference. This workshop enables junior marketers to be successful sooner, by understanding the basic concepts and platforms of their day-to-day jobs and getting the skills they need to become more effective in their roles.

Content Marketing Strategy

Examine all areas of content marketing and the role they play in digital, marketing and business strategies.

Best-practice case studies will walk you through all the components of an effective content strategy. You'll also focus on how to create, distribute and manage your content.

Consumers prefer to be engages with a brand via a story or conversation, so the power of content is immeasurable. Through both in-class discussion and practical exercises, we'll explore how consumer behavior fuels this power and how you can develop your content marketing strategy to be just as powerful. You'll also learn how to properly measure its effectiveness.

Conversion Rate Optimization

Harness the power of conversion and learn how to optimize your site to achieve your online objectives.

This powerful workshop will teach you the fundamentals of how to turn your hard-earned website visitors into leads and sales. Applying the insights you'll get will help you improve your conversion rates leading to increased online revenue and lead generation. If you want to know more about the fast-growing marketing discipline of conversion rate optimization, this is the best workshop for you to dip your toe in the water and get started.

Copywriting (Advanced)

Explore new, clever and engaging ways to push your writing to the next level.

Writing today is an indispensable skill and if you want to excel, you need more than just the basics. Throughout this workshop, you'll engage with and produce strategic and compelling copy that will attract readers.

Copywriting (Essentials)

Discover the essential techniques for writing effective copy.

One of our most popular workshops, copywriting essentials explores the structure, rules and techniques in copywriting. Learn to craft compelling headlines, structure documents and most importantly, engage your reader.

Copywriting for Content Marketing

Plan, write and publish creative content that engages readers and keeps them coming back for more.

During this course, you'll explore copywriting for blogs, PR, social media posts and articles. Discover new techniques and master traditional ones. Explore a variety of effective, compelling and fresh techniques for copywriting for content marketing during this hands-on workshop.

Creative Leadership

Develop senior creative leadership skills to improve business effectiveness.

Winning the promotion and becoming a senior manager

doesn't mean you are ready for all that is ahead of you as you take on more responsibility and manage a team or sets of teams. Becoming a good leader in the new digital economy is not an easy task as there are many opportunities and challenges to tackle every single day. This course will help develop a creative culture, nurture creative talent, help build trusted business relationships that allow you and others to succeed and link business and creative needs with technology and innovation.

Customer Journey Mapping

Ensure customer understanding is at the heart of your marketing.

Create a compelling experience for customers using analytics tools and insights. Customer insights are a crucial part of any marketing strategy or campaign, and yet most marketing strategies are developed with a focus on the product attributes or benefits we want to communicate. In this course, you'll discover the fundamentals of analytics and the different tools that will help you draw insights from data to create a compelling customer experience.

CX for CMOs

This workshop brings together all the critical pieces you need to know in the age of information excess.

CX is not one thing, it's every way the customer experiences your brand and business. This workshop, curated by CMOs, brings together all of the critical pieces that are demanded of CMOs today in delivering customer experience - the holy grail of marketing – giving you real clarity on how to apply these insights to your business.

Data Analytics for Marketers

Engage with data analysis and discover how it can deliver

marketing effectiveness.

This short workshop will help you make sense of the high volume and increasingly complex data available to marketers, as well as build a high-level view of the tools, techniques and processes you might use in the process.

Data Driven Marketing Leadership

Broaden your skill set as a leader and develop a data-driven marketing mindset to support your technical team leaders.

During this workshop, you'll be provided with an outline of how business operations and governance work within the field of data, how to lead and inspire your technical teams and to provide cross-functional management and integration.

Data Driven Marketing Practitioner

Learn how to use data to drive your business forward.

In this workshop, we'll show you how to access both primary and third-party data, develop actionable insights, explore data research and perform analytical techniques. This will help you to tell stories with data, benchmark insights from analytics and incorporate the latest solutions and models to tackle business problems. Our Data-driven Practitioner Workshop is designed for those who have access to data directly and/or who have a team and prefer a self-learning, exploratory approach to learning.

Data Driven Marketing Strategy

Discover how a data-driven marketing strategy can deliver a successful customer-centric marketing presence.

In this workshop, we examine a more strategic approach to using your data. This allows us to uncover information about how customers interact with your brand and identify areas that would otherwise go undetected.

Data Visualization

Establish your own visualization techniques that will help sell your analytics results to business decision makers.

In this workshop, you'll learn how to translate and present analytics in an enticing manner. You'll draw upon insights from data and convert these into commercial insights. This workshop is designed for those who are curious in nature, enjoy problem-solving and prefer a self-learning, exploratory approach to knowledge.

Digital Analytics for Marketers

Introducing an accessible approach to measuring, analyzing and optimizing digital marketing activity.

Learn to apply proven marketing theories to real world examples. Unlock the power of data to enhance decision making and campaign planning. This workshop has been designed so a difficult topic is now simple, straightforward and easy to grasp.

Digital Copywriting Essentials

Discover the essential skills and practices for writing effective digital copy.

Whether it's a quick status update or detailed blog post, writing on a digital platform is already a part of your day. The structures and styles for online are, however, different - there is no one-size-fits-all approach to different platforms. For your copy to cut through the current cluttered digital environment, it needs to be engaging. Through tested techniques, you'll discover the art of writing engaging digital copy for search purposes, emails, websites and social media.

Digital Marketing Campaign Planning & Management

Broaden your skills base by discovering how digital can make your campaigns thrive.

During this workshop, you'll explore the practical elements of digital marketing and how you can integrate them within your brand's activity. You'll learn to determine the right resources, budget, plan and identify opportunities for optimization.

Digital Marketing Channels

Discover how each digital marketing channel can deliver you a customer-centric marketing presence.

In this workshop, we examine each channel individually and uncover information about channel contributions to the consumer journey and how to utilize it in your marketing activity.

Digital Marketing Essentials

Discover industry tips and tricks for successfully incorporating digital channels into your campaigns.

In this two-day intensive workshop, you'll explore the foundations of each digital channel, how they work and how they can fit together to deliver on your marketing objectives. We'll also look at digital tactics, strategies and processes and how you can tie them all together in an effective way.

Digital Marketing Foundations

Broaden your skill set and develop a foundational knowledge of the digital landscape, data, content and customer experience.

During this workshop you'll be provided with an outline of the core foundations and principles of digital marketing. Explore the role of data and content and how this can shape customer experience.

Digital Marketing Strategy

Uncover a framework for successful digital marketing.

Whether it's your business, industry, or campaign, digital continues to have a significant impact on the way we operate. During this workshop, you'll be provided with a framework for crafting a digital marketing strategy. To get the most out of this two-day intensive workshop, you should have a good understanding of the basic digital marketing tactics.

Email Marketing

Boost your email marketing results with proven techniques, technical and strategy improvements.

Explore new ways of using email marketing in your overall communications strategy and learn how to deploy marketing automation techniques to drive customer engagement.

Practical Predictive Analytics

Develop a deeper understanding of predictive analytics.

Using predictive analytics, discover how you can forecast, model and optimize data to create opportunities and prevent loss. To get the most out of this course, you should have a solid knowledge of analytics and have ideally spent some time working in the field - over three years' experience is recommended.

Privacy & Marketing Compliance

A commercial approach to compliance for data-driven marketers and advertisers.

Learn how to protect and enhance your brand's reputation by ensuring your marketing and advertising meets customer expectations and complies with the privacy and marketing content laws.

Programmatic Advertising

Adopt a simple, fresh and effective platform to power your marketing.

Programmatic advertising is reshaping the digital landscape as it's automating everything. Marketers need to exploit the power of automated media trading and learn how they can optimize its productivity. In this workshop, we'll explore various programmatic models and the different technologies available for implementation.

Retention & Loyalty Marketing Strategy

Discover the four pillars to building a comprehensive customer retention and loyalty marketing strategy.

In this two-day intensive workshop, you'll adopt a framework for retaining customers through loyalty marketing strategies. We'll explore the power behind loyalty and advocacy initiatives in both traditional and digital techniques. The proven effectiveness of keeping a customer and nurturing their loyalty and advocacy is where the value is derived.

SEM Essentials

Simple yet successful ways to enhance your search results.

Paid search can transform your business without a huge spend. It's a cost effective, highly convenient channel. See how it can strengthen your search engine marketing, morph into a wider digital strategy for your business and leverage other channels.

Sentiment Analysis

Discover best-practice approaches that use modern text mining and predictive analytics techniques to gain insight into consumer opinions and forecast behaviors.

In this course, you'll advance your knowledge of sentiment and content analysis, and opinion mining, develop a deeper understanding of how to work with unstructured text data (in particular, data retrieved from social media) and learn how traditional machine learning/predictive analytics techniques can be used for the purposes of sentiment analysis. It is recommended that you complete the Practical Predictive Analytics Workshop prior to taking this workshop. This workshop is designed for those who are curious in nature, enjoy problem solving and prefer a self-learning, exploratory approach to knowledge.

SEO Essentials

Find out how SEO drives new customers and better customer engagement.

Score page rankings, better click-throughs, utilize research tools and foster great external links with an effective SEO strategy. Discover what simple techniques can do when applied to your website structure.

Social Media Marketing Essentials

Discover the foundations behind social media marketing and how you can adopt the practices into your own communications mix.

Get up to speed with the latest trends, techniques and technologies in social media and learn to craft your own social media campaign through planning, execution and optimization.

Social Media Marketing Strategy

Research, plan and implement a successful social media marketing strategy from the ground up.

Most organizations and brands are on social media - and if they're not, they should be. Social media is a way for consumers to engage and communicate with brands. But this doesn't mean businesses should just start a Facebook page or Twitter account. It's not that simple, as there are right and wrong strategies to use with each channel. Looking at these channels and their tactics, you'll learn how to develop, implement and measure social media activity.

Community & Customer Relationship Management

- Do you need help improving the efficiency and effectiveness of your marketing management?
- Do you have sufficient time and resources to create and distribute resources to your industry and customer base?
- Are your outreach efforts stagnant or causing disruptions to operations?
- Do you have a potential conflict of interest by handling your ongoing marketing programs with operational resources?

Global Help Desk & Support

- Do you support customers globally, but lack in-house bandwidth and expertise?
- Do you struggle to quantify the value of your marketing program?
- Are you tired of getting blamed for missed opportunities or slow response times?
- Do you have trouble tracking, prioritizing and resolving requests for support?

Marketing Automation Enablement

- Having trouble identifying or selecting marketing automation solutions?
- Do you want more out of your current go-to-market solution?
- Are you in need of consistent communication with your customers?
- Do you lack the budget for technology, but wish you could leverage technology without a capital investment?

Pre-Post M&A Support: Marketing Bridge

- Are you involved in the pre-acquisition due diligence process and concerned with successor liability?
- Do you lack bandwidth or expertise to integrate, oversee or transition a newly acquired company into your marketing program?
- Are you struggling to address customer acquisition risks identified during due diligence?

Agency of Record

- Do you want to grow your marketing team, but lack the budget?
- Do you wish you could leverage the best in industry digital marketing talent without sacrificing equity?
- Are you looking to create a narrative for potential business expansion?
- Do you want access to modular marketing growth without committing to multi-year contracts?

Opportunity Identification & Innovation Management

- Do you need help analyzing the potential savings and benefits from potential customer or product line expansion?
- Do you wish you had time to qualify marketing tools or implement a baseline for business growth?
- Do you have a go-to-marketing plan in place, but lack the staff to manage your day-to-day?

Third Party Vendor Management

- Do you lack the time or resources to audit and ensure your marketing vendors' quality and service performance level?
- Are you tired of correcting errors or performing your vendors' responsibilities?
- Are you unknowingly putting your Company's reputation and compliance at risk by relying on incorrect best practices and roadmap?
- When was the last time you audited your vendor's fees or timeliness of deliveries?

Marketing Program Optimization

- When was the last time you assessed your Company's marketing-related risks, gaps, and challenges?
- Do your processes and procedures reflect your current business requirements and risk tolerance?
- Is your staff configured to support a major marketing migration

www.ingramcontent.com/pod-product-compliance
Lightning Source LLC
LaVergne TN
LVHW041220050326
832903LV00021B/719